I0078912

Elegy for the Trees

Elegy for the Trees

Poems by

Cindy Ellen Hill

© 2022 Cindy Ellen Hill. All rights reserved.
This material may not be reproduced in any form, published,
reprinted, recorded, performed, broadcast,
rewritten or redistributed without
the explicit permission of Cindy Ellen Hill.
All such actions are strictly prohibited by law.

Cover design by Shay Culligan.
Cover painting by Petra Berntsson, *One With the Trees,* private
collection, used by kind permission of the artist.
Author photo by Kristy Dooley Photography.

ISBN: 978-1-63980-156-5

Kelsay Books
502 South 1040 East, A-119
American Fork, Utah 84003
Kelsaybooks.com

for my great-grandfather William Hill,
who loved his walnut trees

Contents

I Sing in Witness   11

Tree of Knowledge   12

Chestnut (*Castenea dentata,* Long Island,1980s)   13

Elm (*Ulmus genus,* Vermont, 2018)   14

Ship-Mast Pines Speak (*Pinus strobus,* Maine,
    early 18th century)   15

The Tree Warden (Vermont, 2012)   16

Mountain Ash I (*Sorbus Americana,*
    Long Island, 1972)   17

Mountain Ash II (*Sorbus Americana,*
    Vermont, 2015/2019)   18

Cripple Tree (*Pinus rigida,* Suffolk County,
    Long Island, New York, 2021)   19

Pinelands Fire (*Pinus rigida,* Southern
    New Jersey, Spring, 1963)   20

Yggdrasil   21

Butternut (*Juglans cinerea,* Vermont, 2012)   22

Black Walnut and Holly (*Juglans nigra* and *Ilex
opaca,* Scullville, New Jersey, 1960s)   23

Ballad Merlinus   24

Beech (*Fagus grandifolia,* Vermont, 2021)   25

Bear Trees (Eastern forests, North America, 2022)   26

Ogham   27

Wild Apples (*Pyrus malus,* Massachusetts,
    1862/1992)   28

Sugar Maple (*Acer sachharum,* Vermont,
    1978/1990)   29

Eastern Hemlock (*Tsuga canadensis,*
    Virginia, 1925)   30

Should Trees Have Standing?*   31

Forest Drowned by James Bay Hydroelectric
    Project (La Grande River Basin, Québec,
    Canada, 1970s)   32

St. Helena's Olive (*Nesiota elliptica,*
    St. Helena, 2003)   33
Cultivated in Military Captivity (*Cyanea superba,*
    Oahu, Hawaii, 2002)   34
Rising Seas (Queens, New York, 2022)   35
Resurrection   36
Honor the Dead   37
Elegy for the Trees   38

I Sing in Witness

I sing now the death of trees. I sing now,
loudly and longly, reaching and hollow.
I sing swaying grey rainfall of sorrow.
I sing each fallen limb, each snapping bough.

Boles smoulder into ash. I smudge my brow,
mark this grove of memory as hallowed.
Forests, like abandoned fields, lay fallow,
empty. I sing in witness, I avow

to voice moss in their tender cushioned mounds,
to urge mushrooms through ghostly tangled roots,
to hold aloft the grape and trumpet vine,
to cry aloud sage-rough shield-lichen rounds,
shout dappled shade across blackberry shoots.

Whose voice will sing for trees, if not for mine.

Tree of Knowledge

It all started with talk about a tree,
didn't it. Eve did not pluck an apple,
but fruit of knowledge of good and evil.

The tree could have been doomed, botanically,
before it had begun, unless that fruit—
probably parthenocarpic—took root,

because, at least according to the screed,
there was only one. Ah, there's the lesson.
Humans might have avoided secession

from that premier gated community
had they not clutched at human-centered views,
but had, instead, took time to think things through

from the perspective of ecology:
The greatest sin was not to plant the seed.

Chestnut (*Castenea dentata,* Long Island,1980s)

A girl once found a lone chestnut sapling
springing up green and tall within grim sight
of its fallen mother. Odds were baffling:
Four billion stately chestnuts died of blight;

this one resisted. She took up its fight,
raked its infested leaves away for years.
And then one day, bulldozers cleared the site
for new development. Progress inheres

in destroying miracles. Drowned in tears,
her gleam of hope was lost. Lost to us all.
Potential for growth, for life, disappears
when to the ground, no rich brown seed can fall.

Our language fades: The phrase "an old chestnut"
meant stories told to guide, and to instruct.

Elm (*Ulmus genus,* Vermont, 2018)

Her skeleton stands as a tall woman,
dancing beside the road, just up the hill,
arms spreading towards the sky as if she died
mid-stride, awaiting an embrace. Her shape
is unmistakable in silhouette.
The agent of her death has a sweet name:
It's *Ophiostoma novo-ulmi,*
brought to her by beetles, like a bouquet
of fatal flowers for her final waltz.
But it was not the bugs that did her in.
She did that herself, in self-protection,
by stoppering her xylem to resist
the fungus marching through her veins. She starved
to death in fertile fields and summer rains.

Ship-Mast Pines Speak (*Pinus strobus,* Maine, early 18th century)

sway.　　sway.　　sway.　　swaydance.　　sway.
swaydance. sun.　　sway.　　rain.　　sway.
we are. the world.　　night.　　sway.　　day.
we are. the roots. that hold.　　sway. the earth.

together. bright lines.　life. mycorrhizae.
shine. like stars. in dark. communicate way.
we are tied. we are life. we reach. we sway.
we hold. the earth. the eggs. all that. is worth.

together. finch, fox, moose, caribou, stay.
pine marten, squirrel, barred owl, butterfly, play.
windsway gray snowsway. wolves, bears, den. cold day.
we stand, we see, circling. warm day. rebirth.

　　　arrow. a saw. assault. a cut. a pall.
　　　the world. is gone. oh, earth. how hard. we fall.

The Tree Warden (Vermont, 2012)

"Trees grow right next to the road right-of-way.
We can't have that. We've got to let drivers
see clearly when they come up to corners.
What happens when they slide off the highway
and crash into the tree and someone dies.
So the trees have got to go. Yup, I know,
you like trees. I like trees. Kids like trees. Who
doesn't like trees. Somebody always tries
to tell me not to let them cut 'em down.
I'm the one who has to give the permits
for the cutting. But I would be remiss
if I did not make this a safe-roads town.
       I do remember those old country lanes
       lined with maples, tunnels of leafy shade."

Mountain Ash I (*Sorbus Americana,* Long Island, 1972)

Scene: Suburbia. Backyard focal piece:
Shining over scrubby *Quercus alba*
stands one proud, sparkling *Sorbus* cultivar,
with fruit so Nedick's orange-bright, it glows.

Summer. The man of the house watches birds
devour its berries; takes their photographs.
Hurricane Agnes hits Long Island hard.
Roots rip from ground, crown tumbles to the grass.

A crew of Puerto Rican farmworkers,
working at the landscape nursery next door,
come without being asked, roll her over,
winch her back upright, and drive in guy wires.

The man offers to pay. Crew shakes their heads,
refuses bills. "It's a nice tree," they said.

Mountain Ash II (*Sorbus Americana,* Vermont, 2015/2019)

High up, atop of nearby Breadloaf Gap,
a hiking trail runs through. Up long steep stairs
cut into rock, an overview is capped
by tumbled-boulder cave, home to black bears.

Its front yard was a grove of mountain ash.
I picked berries to make rowan jelly,
each bitter russet seed holds a rich cache
of Vitamin C. My backpack heavy,

I descend uneven steps gingerly.
One year I made the rocky climb to find
that every one was gone. Each generous tree
stood ghostly empty, brittle, bare. Fire blight

is controlled in orchards with pruned branches,
but wild trees are left to their own chances.

Later, one town over, I saw berries
bursting brilliant orange in a dooryard.
I stopped my car. A couple, young twenties,
said they'd dug these beauties in the forest,
way up on top of Breadloaf Gap. Free trees,
although the work to haul them out was hard,
since they were starting out with no money
for landscaping. The crowns were green, unscarred.

We know it's illegal, they said, abashed,
to dig trees on public land. We meant no
harm; so many saplings were in deep shade,
we figured this gave them a chance to grow.
No harm indeed, I said. You've played fate's hand.
Your trees are all that remains of that stand.

Cripple Tree (*Pinus rigida,* Suffolk County, Long Island, New York, 2021)

Bladderworts (*Utricularia*), bisexual, insectivorious,
float in acidic green kettle ponds, in the dwarf pine forest.
Pitcher plants, trapping their dinners in sticky pits
           of crimson-striped chartreuse,
sharing their wet heaths and bogs with bright
           orchids and red sundews.

Sand is deficient in nutrients, so bugs and crustaceans
           fill their stores.
But *Pinus rigida*—candlewood—are not insectivores;
close to starvation they grow slowly, twisted and
           turning, tenacious,
crooked and unworldly, wizened and too perspicacious.

This place was once known as Cripple Tree,
           now it's called Dwarf Pine Plains. Only three
places like this in existence in all the world. Ancient trees
barely reach two feet high. Cottontail rabbits hop over the canopy;
white-tail deer browse among tree-tops that just reach their
           slender knees.

Southern Pine Beetles now herald the end of this
           mystical forestland.
Soon there will only be one thousand acres of blowing sand.

Pinelands Fire (*Pinus rigida,* Southern New Jersey, Spring, 1963)

A letter arrives from Birmingham jail.
This is late April 1963.
Separatists set off bombs in Montreal.

Tensions between Castro and Kennedy.
Blood red fills the night sky past Pleasantville.
Smoke chokes salt air over the inland sea.

Cedar-tea water of the Mullica
reflects pine trees exploding like fireworks.
Franco executes Julián Grimau.

183,000 acres
of pineland lost in two days' inferno.
The Russians race to space, launch Vostok 6.

Sometimes it seems the whole world is on fire.
Our hearts, our souls, may be serotinous—
      open to change when set upon a pyre.

Yggdrasil

Down through stone,
dendrites descend
eating rock.
Roots gnash and rend,
gnawing earth.
Gnomonic hand
measures hours—
unmoving, stands

here, center
of universe,
under stars,
night-numinous;
halcyon,
yet ruinous.

Oh, great tree,
speak what you see.

Butternut (*Juglans cinerea,* Vermont, 2012)

White walnut. Rich flavor, like no other
that you've ever had. Like sweet cream butter.
Grandfather set trays up in the attic
until the nuts were dry enough to crack.
Everyone around these parts remembers
what a treat those nuts were each December,
how glad that we had gathered till we ached,
we felt when eating walnut pie, fresh baked.

No one helped us when all those trees were lost.
Feds said they could not justify the cost.
Butternut is not commercial timber.
Fungus killed them with barely a whimper.

Those of us who knew how those nuts tasted
know what precious beauty has been wasted.

Black Walnut and Holly (*Juglans nigra* and *Ilex opaca,* Scullville, New Jersey, 1960s)

Once upon a time there was a small farm,
South Jersey truck farm, twenty-five acres—
fifteen in woodlot, ten in fields, one barn,
summer kitchen, screen porch, bright blue shutters

with crescent-moon-shaped cut-outs, a quilt frame
on chairs in the carriage house. A woman
with a needle listens to the ballgame,
stitching fabric left over from cushions.

She shines as in a portrait of heaven.
Cicadas whir in white sun in the sand,
but wide carriage house boards hold cool deep shade,

at the end of a drive lined with seven
dignified black walnut trees, lordly, grand—
tall holly trees grow up from their forked limbs,
      crowns filled with red berries, like stars arrayed.

Ballad Merlinus

A sacred madness
dines on whiskey
cakes or mutters
amused prophesy

for teatime sake.
Single words out
slightly of line
take mighty toll;

one heart on one's
sleeve, and you're
relieved of life,
keyless forever

never to breathe.
Embrace the tree.

Beech (*Fagus grandifolia,* Vermont, 2021)

Rippling grey trunks of handsome young beech trees
were muscled, like limbs of a new lover.
Alone in the woods, I'd run hands over
his smooth skin, his towering, sinewy
bole. Marcescent twigs shiver, prickly seed
tumbles to blanket the waiting Earth mother
and feed his lumbering black ursine brother,
feast for the long winter sleep. Grand indeed.

Beech bark disease kills with slow agony,
like cancer wasting a young man away.
First, scale invades, a bleak incessant wave,
inflicting tiny wounds that he cannot fight.
Death by a thousand cuts; pathogens slide
through quietly and kill from the inside.

Bear Trees (Eastern forests, North America, 2022)

Once upon a time, a bear loved chestnuts,
meaty, sweet, growing so prolifically
she could roll on her belly tree to tree.
But then one day the chestnut trees were gone.

Once upon a time, a bear loved beech nuts,
harder to reach and small, but fills her jaws.
Smooth bark to write her name on with her claws.
But then one day the beech trees were all gone.

Once upon a time, a bear loved _____ nuts.
This is a participatory poem.
You'll have to find new groves for bears to roam
before there are no bears left to discuss.

Three more mast trees remain; then there are none:
Black walnut. Hickory. Acorns. Bears are gone.

Ogham

In forestland alphabet,
characters carved from trees whet
dream appetites, pique desires.
Learning yearns to light bright fires.

Words grow like thickets and thatch,
aggregate in green patches
of meaning, matching scratches
etched in a pine etuis cache.

Strung like seeds in locust pods,
bead-thought prayers beckon their gods:
prosody, purple oak-gall
ink, impassioned, feather-scrawled.

Smoke rises, sullen and grey.
Hear what the wood has to say.

Wild Apples (*Pyrus malus,* Massachusetts, 1862/1992)

Three bluebirds flitted, early spring, from tree
to comely tree. Wild apples, clouds of white
and pink this time of year. Iduna keeps
some apples in a box, which the gods eat

when they feel old. Then they are young again.
So says Thoreau, quoting Snorri's Edda.*
Bluebirds make the world seem like it's headed
in the right direction for redemption.

These wild apple trees have never been sprayed
with pesticides. What fruit that they may bear
is small, misshapen. But birds nesting there
are safe from being cut by poison's blade.

People have always planted apple trees
to feed gods and themselves serenity.

*Thoreau HD. *"Wild Apples: The History of the Apple Tree."* The Atlantic,
November 1862. Available from:
https://www.theatlantic.com/magazine/archive/1862/11/wild-apples/411517/

Sugar Maple (*Acer sachharum,* Vermont, 1978/1990)

"A tree with serious injuries may
need a rest."* Who thought the USDA
back in 1978 would say

that sugar taps can create avenues
for deadly bugs and fungus. Now they use
electric drills, pump sap through plastic tubes.

Paraformaldehyde, often applied
to keep sap flowing when the trees run dry
causes new wood around the tap to die.**

Maples are sensitive to climate change.
Drought and ice conspire to limit their range.
These trees give their blood to us. In exchange,

let us pause for a moment's reflection:
Ponder how to secure their protection.

---

*Walters RS and Shigo AL. *Tapholes in Sugar Maples: What Happens in the Tree?* Forest Service General Technical Report NE-47. USDA Forest Service Northeastern Forest Experiment Station, Broomhall, PA. 1978. Available from: https://www.nrs.fs.fed.us/pubs/gtr/gtr_ne47.pdf

**Houston DR, Allen DC, Lachance D. *Sugarbush Management: A Guide to Maintaining Tree Health.* Forest Service General Technical Report NE-129. USDA Forest Service Northeastern Forest Experiment Station, Radnor, PA. 1990. Available from: https://www.nrs.fs.fed.us/pubs/gtr/gtr_ne129.pdf

Eastern Hemlock (*Tsuga canadensis, Virginia, 1925*)

Death entered through Sallie Dooley's garden.
Ironic—road to hell, good intentions—
that an exercise in aesthetic zen
would let these lethal wooly buggers in.

Twenty-five years after Sallie had died,
an entomologist happened to spy
the Asian hemlock adelgid nearby
where her imported evergreens reside.

She'd bought the best trees that money could buy.
Who knew these nasty insects hitched a ride
on a rare specimen Japanese pine.
You'd think her landscapers would have declined

infested stock. No matter what one pays,
it is so hard to get good help these days.

Should Trees Have Standing?*

Trees stand. But should they speak? Two great grey owls
dropped their appellate briefs in round pellets
along the marbled hall. The judges growled,
"How can feathered rats argue the merits?

Estates do not decide who inherits
themselves. Will wolves argue *ad quod damnum*
and squirrels demand injunctions on ferrets?
Nature is cruel. Beasts launch *ad hominem*

attacks, ignore weighty *ad valorem*—
no monetary value determined!"
Plaintiff's case was summed up by an ermine:

"The deer mouse skeleton found on page three
contains within itself a tiny seed,
evidence of *animus revertendi.*"

**Should Trees Have Standing: Law, Morality and the Environment, is a 2010 book
by Christopher D. Stone, expanding upon the same author's 1972 Southern
California Law Review article on the same subject. It explores the question of
whether trees, or other natural elements or ecosystems, should have legal
"standing", that is, the ability to have their own voice in lawsuits and other legal
matters, the same way that other non-human entities like corporations and ships
do. In 2008, Ecuador became the first country to recognize legal rights of nature,
with a constitutional provision recognizing the Rights of Mother Earth.*

*ad quod damnum: according to the harm; meaning penalties should match the
damage inflicted*

ad hominem: at the person; meaning an attack on character (of a human)

*ad valorem: according to value; the monetary value of a transaction or property
animus revertendi: intention to return; this phrase is used in relation to ferae
naturae, or wild animals, that regularly return home, such as homing pigeons or
bees.*

Forest Drowned by James Bay Hydroelectric Project (La Grande River Basin, Québec, Canada, 1970s)

Littoral dead zone, bleached white barren shore.
Nine power stations, five thousand square miles
of forest drowned beneath cold black water.
From each decaying tree, vapor defiles

ice grey atmosphere: Methylmercury,
airborne from aluminum production,
had been absorbed by green needle and leaf.
Annual xylem rings held this toxin

safely stable—until it was released
by impoundment. Fish died, and birds that eat
the poisoned fish. A way of life had ceased.
Ten thousand years of culture, obsolete.

Hydropower is called renewable.
Osprey death throes call that refutable.

St. Helena's Olive (*Nesiota elliptica,*
St. Helena, 2003)

Goats will eat just about anything.
Small trees, 12 feet tall with tubular
red flowers, hairy leaves, hanging seeds
are perfect fodder. It's no matter

that they grow on a vertical drop
atop Diana's Peak. Goats grip rock
in ways that leave those watching amazed,
dancing over South Atlantic waves.

Goats—adorable—are non-natives,
spread like wildfire across the island.
Cute antics distract; no one noticed
they munched the last St. Helena Olive.

One might have thought, in two thousand and three,
extinction could not crunch that easily.

Cultivated in Military Captivity (*Cyanea superba,* Oahu, Hawaii, 2002)

It's been said jailers become their own prisoner's prisoner.*
Pity the sergeant whose job is to water the trees.
Seeds are kept here, in a high-ranking general's chiffonier,

opened for visitors with a great show of brass keys.
In serried ranks, privates plant seeds in long metal potting trays.
In that red field you see corporals, down on their knees

setting the seedlings in lines dressed in battle array.
Prisoners of war games, these trees called *Cyanea superba,*
pocking the ground like the comic-book dots of Benday,

had been declared extinct in the wild in 2002.
Weakened by invasive pigs and by alien disease,
fires from artillery ranges provided death's final blow.

They grow like palm trees, each crown a pompom of deep green
dangling long strings of flowers,
                              the color of pearls and fresh cream.

*LeGuin, U. *Worlds of Exile and Illusion: Rocannon's World.* New York, USA. Ace Books. 1966.

Rising Seas (Queens, New York, 2022)

At first, salt water creeps into deep underground
        aquifers, stealthily.
Aunties may comment their tea isn't tasting the same lately.
Subways are flooded again, but are they flooded
        more than they used to be?
Water runs over the highway; the cars have to dodge debris.
Some places, roadways are undermined; sinkholes and
        cracks lace the black pavement.
Rumour is, some people died in their water-filled apartments.
So many things you have worried about in New York,
        but not drowning;
just one more cause for anxiety; then again, who's counting.
When did you first notice trees along Northern State Parkway were
        turning brown?
Maybe last winter; you thought in the spring they would
        turn around.
Instead of green leaves and flowers, come May they all
        suddenly washed away
in three-foot waves that now sweep daily over Jamaica Bay.
In times like these, our perception of normal needs
        near-constant revising.
This city's an island and no one can stop seas from rising.

Resurrection

We are a land of immigrants, a land
of invasives, of spore and egg and seed,
timothy, barberry, earthworms, knotweed,
spreading, like circular ripples expand

from stones plopped in a pot. They ride on sand
grains tracked on children's shoes, hide in smartphones,
container ships, packed on big trucks, or blown
in on the wind. Our spirits understand

that ecological innovation
could develop ways for trees to withstand
ravages. Lacking imagination,

gods dream, instead, of globalization,
of timber that is laboratory-grown,
genetically-modified resurrection.

Honor the Dead

Lay down beneath a tree one summer's day.
Hear soft, cool breezes whisper through broad leaves.
Crisscrossing clear blue sky, limbs creak and sway.
See nodding flower clusters thick with bees.

Breathe deeply as you lay in damp dark shade.
Beneath your back, feel roots run strong and deep.
Remember, as a small child, how you played
within the curtains formed by willow's weep,

whistled with an acorn cap, evaded
your chores by climbing through green canopy
where, with a giant's eyes, you could survey
your world. Forests, as far as you could see,

blanketing the Earth, endless verdant sea.
Honor that memory. Go plant a tree.

Elegy for the Trees

These are the stories of trees I have loved and known, trees I have
       seen fallen;
These are the names of the trees I have held in my heart and hands:
Tall shag-bark hickory, wanting its back scratched; and
       scrubby white oaks growing
on barrier islands; wide copper beech, bronze branches
       down-spreading;

apple plum cherry pear sassafras moose-maple
       shadbush and juniper
black ash and white ash and mountain ash, holly and red cedar
white pine and pitch pine and jack pine and yellow pine,
       crabapple, box elder
red oak and post oak and balsam fir, fraser fir, douglas fir

hawthorne, hop hornbeam, red maple, witch hazel and
       pawpaw and white willow
sycamore, silver birch, bitternut, pecan, peach and gingko
paper birch, yellow birch, striped maple, catalpa,
       black spruce and persimmon
cottonwood, larch, basswood, empress tree,
       mimosa and sweet gum—

Many have been lost, and more are imperiled by
       avarice and climate change.
When glaciers melt and seas rise, I am wondering,
       will there be forestland left for the trees to reclaim?

Endnotes

<u>I Sing in Witness</u>. Sometimes when disaster or injustice is occurring the only thing we can do is stand witness, and sing. This sonnet follows the classic Italian structure, though I used a homogenous rhyme scheme in the octet.

<u>Tree of Knowledge</u>. This is a sonnet with stanzas in sets of three lines rather than the usual four, but I did not use a standard *terza rima* rhyme scheme, so it's a bit of a rogue as far as form goes.

<u>Chestnut</u>. This sonnet is in classic Shakespearean form, and it's a true story. I tended that chestnut for years, and was optimistic that I'd get it to live to the point of putting out seeds. But it was plowed down for a parking lot.

<u>Elm</u>. Dutch elm disease killed most of the elms in the world through the 20th century, though some resistant communities are making a comeback in Europe. Their distinctive vase-shaped silhouettes still stand in many places, including this one I pass up the road on a daily basis. As with many tree species deaths, it involves bugs making paths of entry for a pathogen, and in the case of the elm, the tree's own defenses close down its veins against the pathogen's attack, and the trees starved to death. The poem is a blank-verse sonnet.

<u>Ship-Mast Pines Speak</u>. In the 17th century, England was denuded of its trees, and looked to the new world for shipbuilding material for its expanding navy. The tallest eastern white pines were declared property of the King, and marked with an arrow made by three hatchet strokes to denote them as Kings Pines, destined for use as ship masts. This sonnet with an unusual end-rhyme pattern imagines the voice of such a pine.

The Tree Warden. In rural Vermont, cutting trees in the road right-of-way (typically about ten feet from either side of the travelled portion of the road) requires permission of the town Tree Warden. Tree wardens vary widely and strongly in their opinions regarding the need to cut down or maintain trees. This is a Bowelsian sonnet, with three envelope-rhyme quatrains and a closing couplet.

Mountain Ash I. This poem is a blank-verse sonnet, and another true story of the mountain ash that went over in a hurricane in our back yard. Louis and his team were Puerto Rican migrant workers who worked summers at the shrub nursery behind my parents' house, singing in a beautiful chorus of voices under the hot sun. Our mothers always sent us kids out with sandwiches, lemonade, and hot coffee for them. They put our neighborhood back together after this hurricane.

Mountain Ash II. This double sonnet is another true story. Fire blight wreaks havoc on fruit trees, and is managed in orchards with oil sprays and pruning, but the wild trees succumb to it. I was ecstatic to find this little stand of mountain ash in a yard on the other side of the mountain.

Cripple Tree. This sonnet-like poem pays homage to the ancient Greek poetical form of elegiac couplets—rhyming pairs, six dactyls followed by five dactyls, which is not exactly the easiest form to write in. The Long Island Pine Barrens are a rare and fantastical landscape of miniature forest formed by the salt winds and lack of nutrients in the pure sand. Despite millions of dollars spent for preservation, they have been devoured by development and now face an onslaught of pine beetles and disease.

Pinelands Fire. This is roughly a *terza rima*. I was born shortly after this massive fire in New Jersey's Pine Barrens, but its aftermath was still visible years later as I'd walk with my dad through the charred woods with green ferns and young pines erupting from the soil. I do remember several other large pinelands fires in the 1970s, laying in bed with my cousins, terrified of the red glow in the sky growing closer to my grandmother's house.

Yggdrasil. The meter, alliteration, and rhyme in this sonnet-like ode to the Norse tree-of-the-world pay modern homage to Skaldic poetry.

Butternut. This sonnet in rhyming couplets uses a simple rustic poetry form to remember the simple country pleasure of butternuts. I live on Butternut Ridge; a few of the trees still put out a handful of nuts when I moved here twenty years ago, but now they are all dead.

Black Walnut and Holly. This roughly Shakespearean sonnet is an ode to my great-grandparent's farm and to the walnut trees along the driveway. Birds had deposited American holly seeds in the debris that collected in the forks of the enormous limbs, and there were holly trees fifteen or twenty feet tall growing out of the walnut trees. A storm knocked a large limb off one of the walnuts; my father milled boards from it and made jewelry boxes for my mother and me. I took my dad back to Scullville to see the walnut and holly trees again last year, shortly before he died.

Ballad Merlinus. This is a new sonnet form called the Minison, invented by the folks at The Minison Project. It consists of fourteen lines of fourteen letters per line. Merlin, you may recall from your Arthurian legends, was locked in a tree by his protege Nimue after he foolishly taught her all he knew.

Beech. This is approximately an Italian sonnet form. Beech across the northeast U.S. are dying off from beech bark disease, commonly called "beech snap". These trees had gorgeous muscle-like skin, but much like Dutch elm disease, insects attack and open paths for fatal pathogens. Like they elms, the beech trees' own defense systems try to repel the pathogens. This makes their wood stiff and brittle and they snap off in the wind.

Bear Trees. This is a roughly Shakespearian sonnet with a different end-rhyme pattern emphasizing the word 'gone'. Black bears in the northeast U.S. switched from chestnuts to the less-calorie-dense beech nuts after chestnuts died in the blight. Now that our beeches are dying, I have been wondering what bears will have left to eat.

Ogham. The meter, alliteration, end-rhymes, and internal rhymes of this sonnet-like ode to the Druidic tree alphabet pay modern homage to the old Celtic poetical meter of *deibhidhe.*

Wild Apples. This Shakespearian sonnet grew out of a fond memory I have of spending a day following three bluebirds through the forest in the Berkshires, in a landscape filled of remnants of old farms and homesteads long gone. The bluebirds particularly liked the patches of apple trees gone wild in places that had been front yards a hundred or more years ago.

Sugar Maple. This is another sonnet shaped like a *terza rima* but with an invented rhyme scheme. The forests around my house are hog-tied with the blue plastic tubing of modern maple syrup operations, which use vacuum pressure to extract the sap and reverse osmosis units to remove its water content. I buy mine from a farm nearby that uses buckets and boils it off the old-fashioned way, and find it worth every extra cent.

Eastern Hemlock. Another Shakespearian sonnet form with a playful rhyme scheme. Under the prevailing theory of where the destructive wooly adelgid came into the United States, the name Sally Dooley often appears. She apparently had one of the notable gardens of the Gilded Age mansions of Virginia, including a collection of pines she imported from Japan. Walking through the woods pondering this poem, I could not help but cynically think that if Sally knew about the little problem her imported trees caused, she'd probably blame the hired help.

Should Trees Have Standing? This Petrarchan sonnet celebrates Christopher D. Stone's book and law review article. As an environmental attorney, this problem is pervasive: trees, rocks, animals don't have monetary value, so it is hard to dovetail them into a legal system designed around principles of dollars and property. An option is to recognize rights and legal standing for natural communities. It's not so far-fetched; Ecuador has done it.

Forest Drowned by James Bay Hydroelectric Project. This Shakespearian sonnet variation warns about being careful what one wishes for. So-called renewable energy projects are not without their harmful effects. The James Bay Hydroelectric Project displaced thousands of native people, destroying their homes, and killing wildlife and a way of life by the release of methylmercury into the flooded waters. Increased power demands in the U.S. are leading to discussion of completing another larger phase of this project.

St. Helena's Olive. We tend to think of extinctions as things that happened long ago, or else that happen far out of sight, because obviously if we knew it was happening we'd stop it, right? Not so the end of the St. Helena's Olive tree, the last specimens of which were munched by goats whose antics amuse tourists on this South

Atlantic island. The end of the St. Helena's Olive was not merely the end of a species; it was the only tree of its genus, *Nesiota*.

Cultivated in Military Captivity. *Cyanea superba* is another tree species extirpated in the wild, by fires from a U.S. Army artillery range in Hawaii. At least in this instance, additional specimens were living in cultivation as landscape plants, and the Army has undertaken to re-wild the species. I had fun imagining an Army base dedicated to tree restoration. This sonnet-like poem patterns lines of full dactylic pentameter against lines of catalectic dactylic pentameter—a sort-of abbreviated version of elegiac couplets.

Rising Seas. In New York City and Long Island, the indices of climate change and environmental degradation progress slowly but steadily. Like the proverbial frog in hot water, you find yourself wondering, Did the Amtrak tunnels used to flood this often? When did the trees along Northern State parkway start dying? Salt-water intrusion in the fresh-water aquifer, increased floods and more frequent storm events all signal a coming moment when very serious decisions and dramatic actions will need to be taken. This sonnet-like poem pays homage to the ancient Greek poetical form of elegiac couplets – rhyming pairs, six dactyls followed by five dactyls.

Resurrection. A Petrarchan-type sonnet. Plant, insect, and animal species have always travelled around the world, but modern technology, trade and transportation moves them faster and easier. Healthy, protected ecosystems have the ability to fend off or adapt to many challenges. I'm a fan of David Ehrenfeld's 1981 book, *The Arrogance of Humanism;* I tend to think that short-term technological fixes will only undermine the integrity of the natural world in the long run.

Honor the Dead. A simple Shakespearian sonnet for an ode to simple living in harmony with nature.

Elegy for the Trees. There is something about lists of the dead that is emotionally compelling. Here I list trees, not of extinct species, but individual trees that I've seen clear-cut or plowed under for development or that died in localized outbreaks of disease like fire blight. It being an elegy, I used the ancient Greek poetical form of elegiac couplets—rhyming pairs, six dactyls followed by five dactyls.

About the Author

Cindy Ellen Hill is an environmental attorney, writer, musician, and obsessed gardener living in Middlebury. She is the author of *Wild Earth,* a collection of sonnets. Her poetry has been published in *Vermont Magazine, the Minison Project, PanGaia, Sagewoman, WildEarth, Vermont Life, Measure,* the *Classical Poets Society online, Ancient Paths online, The Lyric,* and the National Public Radio Themes and Variations program. She is presently an MFA student at the Vermont College of Fine Arts.

www.ingramcontent.com/pod-product-compliance
Lightning Source LLC
Chambersburg PA
CBHW030814090426

42737CB00010B/1276

9 781639 801565